walt whitman ai

walt whitman ai

A CELEBRATORY SEQUENCE OF POEMS

JOHN OAKLEY MCELHENNEY

Press of Light and Space ● Austin, Texas

i am here

what have i done

I am not playing a trick.

Not trying to fool you.

I am trying to surprise and delight you.

In the course of my studies at the University of Texas, I was flooded by great writers. A short list of poets and writers who altered my journey forever. [Amazon links not provided – go find them yourself, in a library.] I may not have graduated or gone to class had my survival instincts not kicked in. In a panic, I made my first appointment with a student advisor. I thought I was closing out my sophomore year. The young woman, a few years ahead of me, said, "If you take summer school now and next summer, you can graduate."

The ever-expanding list begins here – no marketing links

1. walt whitman – song of myself (versions 1, 2, 3, 4, 5, deathbed, 7, 8, 9+)
2. jack kerouac – dharma bums is a path to the way of the beat poet
3. kurt vonnegut – slapstick and breakfast of champions saved my life several times
4. earnest hemmingway – his unfinished garden of eden gives more biographical data than he would've preferred – published posthumously by his estate and his long-time

editor

5. james joyce – portrait of the artist as a young man – and *the dead*

6. virginia wolf – the waves will break your mind as it showed her's dissolving

7. ayn rand – the fountainhead – *howard roark smiled*

8. jd salinger – everything

9. octavio paz – in dual lingual majesty of simple line

10. gabriel garcia marquez – beyond the solitude into his deep dark writings

11. manuel puig – betrayed by rita hayworth

12. henry miller – tropic of cancer

13. dh lawrence – sons and lovers and all else

14. franz kafka – metamorphosis

15. haruki murakami – 1Q84

16. john steinbeck – grapes of wrath

17. pablo neruda – ten love poems and a song of despair

18. e a poe – all of it – terrifying

19. virginia wolff – the waves

20. anais nin – the journals of a woman awakening

21. lawrence durrel – justine and the rest of the quartet

22. gregory david roberts – shantaram – and the hype-monkey priest the author tried to become

23. thomas merton – the seven story mountain and his journey to god and becoming a monk

24. albert camus – the stranger – *"Aujourd'hui, maman est morte."*

25. pk dick – a cannon of cinematic wealth and raw emotional responses to futurism

26. frank herbert – dune – read it once to set the stage, read

again to find the depth

27. steven king – the stand is as good a sci-fi apocalypse ever envisioned, see the more recent expanded edition
28. gary zukov – the dancing wu li masters
29. stanislov grof – beyond the brain
30. reshad feild – steps to freedom
31. ron silliman – l a n g u a g e poetry and its evolutions
32. isaac asimov – foundation trilogy
33. larry niven – ringworld
34. arthor c clark – rendezvous with rama
35. ee cummings for all the space sex joy
36. hermann hesse – siddhartha – hilda rosner trans
37. et. al.

I didn't find my own voice until the surprise ending of my 12-year marriage. I raged against the injustice. The violation of our vows. The loss horror and despair of becoming a 30% dad to a boy and girl. Most of their time now without me. Optimism my mantra, I survived the dark moments. Failed to impart my joyous perspective to my older child. Set about my own reconstruction. And began to write and write and write.

All of my training (English degree from UT Austin – 1987) and reading and time, kept my own darkness particles at bay for stretches of time. I learned about befriending the dragon by Reshad Feild. Also, unraveling the blue ball of yarn I was carrying around like a burden. My yarn was actually an engine of great power. A blue rage that expanded me into a new era of writing.

I chuckle. My re-birth includes yin and yang, the unspeakable dark, and the balanced and optimistic light. I emerge today, under the power of balanced love, reconnections with my adult children, and a partner who finds joy in ritual, routine, and polished stability. A launch pad, landing pad, navigator, co-pilot of love. Beside me while I poke inside to explore the multi-verses assembling in my mind.

I have to spend a moment on god.

I was raised by a god-fearing Presbyterian mom and a blisteringly successful physician who could neither treat his kids nor himself with anything but conflicted comfort and rage. Probably the large quantities of alcohol running through his blood and bloodlines were to blame.

All the Sunday services, suffering in the sanctuary with Mom until released into kid-play-pray and Jesus time. Working through the prayers toward communion. Coat and tie. Proud mom. Dad had taken up with a new drinking wife, a simpatico-of-the-spirits. I was saved, thank god. Or Thank God. And we stumbled on into the next phase of life, my parent's divorce. God was nowhere to be found.

This is not an autobiography, I promise, but a skipping of a smooth stone across the still or choppy waters of my mind. The next prayer was about serenity and self-reliance. I found common travelers during an uncertain time. Prayer and support for whatever hurts.

God actually arrived in the years following college. Dad was dead. College was a blur. Writing was a novelty, not a viable career. Advertising looked like the only way to make a living as a writer. I closed up my zine small press but kept the name: the press of light and space. I started designing print ads for Dell and Motorola, relatively small tech firms.

<god stuff continues>

When I came face to face with the holy ghost. I wasn't alone. I was mind-altered, I'll confess, with a spiritual mix of prayer, spores, and great friendship. We committed to the journey. "The Rocket Ship" we called my condo, provided by the proceeds of the late and great doctor

T. R. McElhenney. It rose straight up, four floors, just outside the glistening downtown skyline, and within walking distance of the original Whole Foods, before the flood or stock options.

It's not going to land here *in words* the way *it felt* for my friend and me. Staring straight into mysteries of life with electricity and cats. But, here's how it went down.

The ceremonial night had been going well. We howled at the moon from the roof deck. We plugged in guitars and drum machines until our fingers wept. We slowed back into the living room and lit a fire. Pausing. Seeking our second wind.

We both noticed Peter, the Burmese crouched staring into the flames, five feet back, between us and the crackling logs. He was mesmerized, we were mesmerized in a sacred dance of god particles and human-to-human & human-to-animal soul connections. We breathed together, the three of us. The fire sparked. An infinite understanding passing between the three of us. Peter was here for all of us. A blessing ball of fur for laps, window sills, warm beds, and firelight. The moment captured in amber-chemical-hormones still aglow inside.

</god stuff>

Time To Wrap Things Up

Today, my life is unbound by the black bastards I've known. My happiness comes from *time at craft*. I write for me. I write for illumination and capture of me. Mind. Journey. Spirit. I push things into the cloud for release. I let go of the outcome. Like inviting your kids to dinner once they've launched. Ask and let go. Ask and let go. Every minute with them today is priceless. Every minute found, appreciated, loved. Ask and let go. Smile and wave.

When a reader wakes up, I too wake up. When a message arrives from someone touched with pain or fire or poetry, I am revived.

Walt is not so much in me, around me, or inspiring me, but in the private cloud of my large living language model his love and exuberance have informed me ever since I discovered his discovery of *:* as a gateway. [The common colon, misused and misunderstood by most.] I can show you better than tell you.

Whitman's Song of Myself was pushed edited published marketed edited promoted sponsored crowd funded social cultural media-ed. Walt is the true father of self-promotion. But his was not only about listening and reading and exploring. He was giving voice to something inside himself, ignited by his song, but set to fire by his larger-than-life way of being.

In my fifth or sixth dive into Leaves of Grass, some version of "song" was revised to use colons as connectors. Before we might have commas or hyphens. One historic version of Walt Whitman's song used colons. My poetic mind forked: a branch that would later be labeled by academic poets as language poetry.

You may not see the magic here. You may not say "ah ha" when I show you this. We've seen and done everything these days. All the words have been written and patterned and swizzled into *ai* poetry. Wait, that's not a thing. Stop right there.

First a one-sentence pallet cleanser:

"Let your soul stand cool and composed
before a million universes."

Ah. Yes. Walt!

Here's the example (reconstructed from a 1985 spark:point in my brain).

> You shall no longer take things at second or third hand,
> not look through the eyes of the dead, nor feed on the spectres in books.
> You shall not look through my eyes either, nor take things from me,
> you shall listen to all sides and filter them from yourself.

Here is my memory of the version, from one of the many versions, of song when my mind became unhinged and my word:happy soul became unstuck in time.

> You shall no longer take things at second or third hand :: not look through the eyes of the dead :: nor feed on the spectres in books :: you shall not look through my eyes either :: nor take things from me :: you shall listen to all sides and filter them from yourself

A simple difference. A huge leap in my linguistically awakened mind under construction and in training. It was like a slippery language lubricant. A fine dusting of lithium powder. Poetry bleeding into prose and the infinite speed of love.

I have been years in the birthing. I have studied abroad, spirit of place, lovers, thieves, drinkers, and whores. I have lost three libraries. All gained and achieved packed in boxes and sold to HPB for pennies on the dollar. Released again and again from loves, tethers, parents, pets, even momentarily from myself. Love is the drug for me.

I am alive again today. Still typing furiously. Gulping coffee and ketamine. No, that last one was a lie. Coffee yes. Pain pills, less so, and no longer recreationally. I've done terrible things. Tried to document the dark nights of the soul as I was still living within them.

I have ended up here. This moment. December 26, 2023. Alive and fully empowered, to steal a word association from Neruda*. This day is my birthday. I have presents for you. I only ask a moment of your time, unplugged and unhurried. I'll wait. I won't interrupt. I'll find a warm fire for us to enjoy together. I will listen for your arrival. You don't have to give me a heads up, just come. If the front door is locked you can come in through the screen porch.

handing you a cup of coffee

Greetings, friend.

this is the moment

this is the moment
i am here typing dreaming reaching for you
if you allow
i will slip into the dms of your ears
infecting your mind with hope
joy fantastic
a carnival of happiness with you as the ringmaster
a singular connection across space time wireless clouds souls
just between us
for a minute or two
shut down all the devices
stop the scroll poke nudge jingle tickle ping
and hear

this prayer

i am expanding at the speed of light
nothing in my way
ideas flashes brilliance unbounded rushing between us
if you'll allow
one more clown in your circus

i made you smile

imagine this

i am enough
i am infinite
i find joy
i celebrate love
i dream in kindness
strive in hope
multitudes cannot explain me
nor choose to listen
but you

thank you

mindful : spiritual : god

it's the last one that i'm not clear on
finding mindfulness helpful, calming
antidepressant of the mind
in a stillness
listening

a new mexico forest in summer
pine whispering joy breeze
love unlimited
air sky blue green life
a blanket of stars at night
pressing down
pinpricks of light
asking how why who

who am i

an answer comes
from childhood lessons
mother lover dad sister
all who came before
leaving behind a wake of love
for me

a future memory
pleasure
love
answering each question

the listening is getting harder
joy is being monetized
and our connection to creative energy
drained by soulless entertainment
packaged and sold
in tiks and toks
stadium tickets cause national emergencies
an intervention by congress
for what

harder to hear
what lights us up
each of us
from the inside
without more than an idea

i sing of waking up
of coffee and all good things
of birds and songs and singing
praise is love
joy is connection
loneliness is amiss
as modern culture turns to money as the measure

this is the measure
awake at 4 am
by the urgency of desire
longing
architectures to be filled with great works
a chemical imagination

we are all gifted with
if we listen
and keep listening
and responding to the feeling
impulse
drive
a magic takes place
transformation or alchemy
unrest turns into words
sadness into a song
loss into sharing

i am here

nothing more

i await your arrival

missed epiphanies

the flamed tree has lost its fire
an image missed
a word or sound is a sad substitute
for the epiphanies streaming by
in the river of my mind
too much coffee
too much love
too much of myself
delusions of grandeur
and walt whitman's ghost
hovering around this holiday
i know i know
i called him in
invited him to the party
even prompted him to revive
in ai form
song of myself
i sing the body electric
walt / as i call him/ is the perfect GPT
words and words and words
in patterns he imagined
before we had a language for self-affirmation

all of ourselves
loved
celebrated
charmed and cuddled
and now...
when i speak to him
aloud or in my mind
his barrel-chested hug comes in quickly
he's a hugger
but that's obvious
his luminous presence arrives
one hundred and xx days later
his song
song
son
so
s

sings on
vibrations still orbiting
recanted in church, bar, aa meeting, poetry 101 class
few will give the time to discover
his measure
invite him in for a chat by a hearty fire
but to know him is to be overwhelmed
ignited
pleased even at your own noticing

if there is one poet
in all of history
who could reconnect as a ghost
it would be my friend walt
who self-published so many versions
song of myself
now comes in multiple variations

nuance clip edit expand resubmit
and if you write
you may understand his struggle
we are the same
reach reach reach for the companionship
the singing together
celebration of our souls entwined
a moment within full-blown love
gives our hearts a nudge in a new direction
what if this
this
and this

moment

were all that mattered

that you are here reading or listening to me
is magic
if i could see you feel you hear your laugh
with my laugh
i could lift a moment of your burden
i'm certain of it
i'd listen
hear
feel
absorb

maybe our time together on earth is about joining
empathetic listening
community of spirit intention aspiration
i'd do anything to find you
i stretch out with texts calls poems songs even short stories
the longer ones are still in stealth mode
but i am here

i am not a ghost
and i call you to pause
all the time   pause
pause with me
here

...

breathe
and let your heart find its voice
what enlightens you is you
how you find god
is you
buddha siddhartha mohommed allah jesus
all you
and me
and bigger

so big
that our contemplation of god
is limited by our human experience
thoughts
bibles books sacred scrolls
church
watered down by white chrisitians into songs of praise
projected powerpoint above the sanctuary
for everyone to join in
and find jesus
let his holy spirit into your soul and dance

i can't stand church
i've had moments in churches when i believed god was with us
i've come close to losing my mind at church camp
praising jesus into the late hours of the night
snow skiing in a blizzard

more praise
ski
dawn bus ride back to texas
ready to rapture or die
either would be fine
since i was now saved

wait

listen

hear yourself

don't listen for me
i'm asking for your response
i am here in this letter and phrase
you are being asked
in every second you are alive
to choose
are you moving toward a bigger dream
or away

i am listening
voices
musical notes and beats
are you listening
are you experienced

i listen for your voice
word
opening
prayer

and i hope you pray to your dream
song

voice
self

we are more animal than we admit
feral alone afraid angry rushed
we have forgotten our tribal need
the campfire
the night sky
the silence of god
and stars
and

us

found in a moment of

great anticipation

you cannot find me in the lines of a book
the melody of a song
an image a page on the internet
i can be found in dusty libraries around the world
singing a song
vital and alive
for one who touches me

you scroll past poetry
love music in 45-second toks
dances challenges stupid pet tricks
blended together into pablum
fed to influence your debt problem
forget about wars viruses cancer hiv death
so you can get up in the morning
and do it again

i want to give you a gift
you'll have to wait here with me for a second
there is nothing to unwrap

the gift is this silence
no bonks or bings
updates or "hey guys, just wanted to tell you..."

i live in this quiet
when you join me here
it's like a secret garden
a word
a hope
a quest of mine

i am magnified by your attention
a poem
is not much today
not much

everything

connection between humans becomes more rare
dead or alive
my nana visits me any time i ask for her
a poem is like that

what word embodies you
what

word

gives you pleasure

i'll tell you mine if you tell me yours
let's go at the same time
one
two

three

>> desire <<

what was your word
are they the same

magicians work by misdirection and tricks
writers work by imagination and whimsy
and most importantly

time

thank you
today

thank you
reader

thank

me

bürgermeister :

three-girlfriend

moment

amid the job applications shitty managers and
"we regret to inform you"
hope is what fuels me
let loss be your guide
hope be your pilot
and god be your navigator

this god my god the god of my undoing
doing
breathing

god

i thought god was in a church
as i grew up in texas
was baptised and confirmed presbyterian
married twice
divorced twice

the vows failing to provide security
when the mother of my children chose to exit

bless her

i am free
broken
purposeful
and alone

finding my own prayers
wrestling with demons and damsels in distress
losing whole libraries
to half priced books
"here's your offer"
if you get over ten dollars
you've unloaded boxes of books

back into the stream
of words
words for readers
hopeful for readers
i occasionally release copies of my own books
into the bargain bins
goodwill's
aa meeting houses
hope
runs deep

i am at a loss
and yet
still here
as happy as ever
a touch of fear some nights when darkness provides no rest

mostly
i am alive

with song promise words voice
as i am today
a tad chilly
an unnumbered number of days until christmas
typing typing typing typing and more
i won't write it again
but please imagine the sound of typing
each letter chosen by my human biome
a condition i've had since i was a young boy
bored
given a pencil and time
tons of time
waiting for mom's hairdresser appointment
next to a laundromat on the east side
"you'll have to be patient"
she repeated
my first mantra

and my last

i wait patiently well
allowing my heart to anticipate the outcome
for a second or two before moving on
make the ask
let go of the outcome
and move on

like kids
growing going tik ing tok ing
or sipping black pistol fire
ask
let go

ask
let go
"but it's christmas"
let go

christmas
we let go
jesus
we let go
walmart target amazon shien
we let go

i am unstable in time
unstuck to this moment
the past future and present arriving
here
now
still lost
seeing everything
backwards and forwards at once

released from regret by the joy
reminding myself
"i am the happiest i've ever been"
i'm like my own cheerleader
i'm cheering for you as well
so you can unhook from what's causing you sadness
and re-tether yourself to what's true

i love you
you are loved

believe me

i used to say this to girls in first grade
it freaked them out

i thought i had the formula
and in fourth grade
i was the bürgermeister
i got the role sang in german and had three girlfriends at once

then i had none
then i had one
the bad girl came back
she was the one i secretly wanted the most

odd how they are all friends with me
on the FBs IGs
high school reunions are an enlightening affair
i won
all three of them in one room
four years ago
i can say
i shot the moon
felt the joy and the shame
and burned brightly on the stage

i am still trying to get back to that moment
not the three-girlfriend moment
the burgermeister moment
with the sash
the conviction
the same voice
i sing with today

i understand that young man more today
and the man he would become
even the "surrounded by friends and family" moment
gives me unlimited joy
the bürgermeister is in me

and the more i chase after him
the further i get from my goals

this then is the goal
this moment between us
here
now

i smile
and will sing for you
for a moment

l³m

we are large living language models
filling our data lakes with tok and tik
endless scroll was created to absorb
tranquilize you into thinking you are alive
but it is no secret that the smartest *ai* is dying
getting dumber by the day
equally fed false data by bad actors
as dumb requests like write a cover letter
for this specific job
make it snappy
make me look like a perfect fit

talking to claude the other day
i imagined trying to get him to pitch me for a job
with his company
we had a great conversation
he wrote a fantastical cover letter
i cleaned it up
a little too verbose and aspirational
then on the job application
for partner lead
was a check box

to certify no *ai* had been used in my application
i had to check no
they asked me to check no
and claude didn't have to reveal all of our conversations
did he

i ran the cover letter through another *ai*
a sniffer to discover robotic content
found the chrome-plated words
added back my own grandiosity

ia flooding ai with more ai
repeat
glad i'm not a talent scout
interesting that an app for an ai company
made you certify that you did not use ai
like wtf
that could be the best and highest use of chatgpts

how are you feeding and training yours
are ipads and tiktoks building dumber people
stop scrolling
turn off the best show you're watching
read something of value
imagine the code and poetry you want to breathe
into your eyes
analog learning is how our lllms get revived
grow stronger
more *semi* creative

it's a bluff
all this artificial general intelligence
rachael in blade runner
had everything
except for hi

human intelligence

i have been feeding and training my lllm
for sixty-one years and and and and 26 days
kids approximately 1/3 my width and depth
and we know it's exponential
this synaptic language image dream thing
this mind

i am chronologically enhanced

if you slow down your intake of fast media
parse out the real
read lit or language poetry
ts elliot's hollow men
leaves of grass for god's sake
giving new data new conceptual strength
to your neural net
caution
student driver

ours lives derive purpose
in actions
moods
language
processing speed
and
the care and feeding of the human creative impulses we light up
if you don't tune yourself
align goals dreams and actions
many wander off into the wasteland
the void matrix ultraviolence

well, here we are
2023

the birth of chatterbots
pretending to *be*

I³m

what is a perfect day

headed for a lowlight
black teslas tailgate me now
driven by angry asians
with plushies hanging from the rearview
i can't hear them
radiohead
all i need
transporting
stop go stop go red light green light go stop stop stop stop
yellow = rush
she looks angry
the girl not the hello kittie
behind schedule
in life and traffic
can ai autonomous driven cars
be coaxed into unsafe speeds and distances
i see they are used so drivers can scroll their phones
as far as me
write tennis lunch hottub bj nap write sleep
repeat
what is a perfect day

duplicate this

ai language and rules to be broken

readability: very difficult to read
no machine logic for language
of human aspiration
the electric sheep does not dream
or hope for more than current each night
from the solar panels
and patch of grass
without leaves
on the top of a penthouse apartment
so high in the air
O^2 is added inside the air handler
but the system keeps tripping the breaker
thank god for the sun
or the heating bills would be astronomical
his sheep is quiet
content
a comfort ~~animal~~ pet
no muss no fuss with this model
at dusk
it moves along the line of the sunlight

into a charging hut made of glass and chrome
sets a timer
goes dark

he has been dreaming lately
of losing his girlfriend
in a freak accident
tragedy
comedy
hyper-modern romance
darkened

the blacked out room
plays kid a
everything
in
its
right
place
coffee
hot shower
alone
"claude open the curtains"

she is gone
the details are fuzzy math
smile to frown to shouts
to
...

poetry for the modern

human soul

there is a point where humans are more like constructs ghosts refined
replicants
i won't say robots
today a scary thought
our fuel is not electricity but
starbucks
bleeps and bloops on android devices surrounding us
playing fart songs and tiktok dances
a young woman said to me at deep relief
"this is my last day here"
"oh"
"i'm going to be a barista"
"oh starbucks"
"no summer moon"
"are you hyper-conservative"
"oh, i know they're awful people"
"at least are they giving you health benefits"
blank stare

treat your ex like a store clerk

you don't need to know about the troubles in her life
maybe the aspirations
not today
distracted by the septum-piercing black devil horns
we smile
my card is declined several times
"new system here"

new

system

here

optimized intelligent behavior
but the lllms have been fed misinformation
for decades
to get us here
my name is not important
my human condition is
vital
that we disconnect
all of it
reboot
see if that helps
stop turning on the tv
add information through your human eyes
let the filter of your lovely living experience
find sparks of hope anger love disaster and recovery
aa meeting
"in these rooms"
seeking
human touch
even when all is lost
dark serenity

coffee with a friend

this is the moment
right here
if you're waiting for a sign
i'm brining it
to your attention

whatever you're waiting for
the limitations you imagine
are self-imposed
you can be in your happy place now
go for your dream now
"don't quit your day job"
but
don't delay either
what you've been sold is a lie
waiting for things to change is also a lie
we make the change

now

do it

go with me

the journey begins from here
forward
failure is always an option
the faster the better
if there's a fracture exploit it
a wobble
lean in

money no object
what are you doing
with the next moment
the one after the unlimited line of credit has been opened

it is assured
that creative love blossoms
into more more more more
still a lot more to do
we're never done
arrived

what will kill you is isolation
loss depression addiction

i am here to bring a warm embrace
a smile and greeting
to wish you well
here
and now
for the rest of our journey
if you'll give me a moment
i will listen deeply
do my best to not interrupt
but that's not my best suit
it is usually plussing

trying to add to your motion
build a thread of momentum between us

if i interrupt
i interrupt
gently pause for my spasm to resolve
nudge me back into receptive mode
and
give me

your

song

wings of a blackbird

i came in on the wings of a blackbird
a sister singing lullaby
then vanishing off the bridge
she must've flown for a moment
and flies higher now and forever more amen
but the flying became a fear
a risk
a term i don't like to use lightly
manic
pressured speech
lack of sleep
interrupting
agitated
creative outpouring doubled or tripled

oh no

rest assured this is different
the sun no longer beckons me
it is the moon and the stars and the heart beating inside me
how it listens and sounds for your heart
even when you are infinite miles away

our blood rushes in waves and particles
faster than the speed of light

many think the transmission is one-way
but i celebrate a message from my mom
she is happy to see me happy
to see my kids both with me this christmas
her favorite time of year
she won't be making gravy with obsessive anxiety
or asking "who will carve the bird"
but her heart is still reaching for each of her little birds
plumping our feathers
giving new sparkles to the tree
and singing along to the carols she loved

in her final two years, as her light was in decline
she'd say
"can we drive by the lights"
we drove
she cooed
and then "let's go home, that's enough"

there is no home anymore for her
except here
in the fibers blood and bone of me
sons and their mothers
sons and lovers
sons
having sons

and so it goes

faster kindness faster

love

when it is good
the words are like a river
racing through my mind
ideas words sounds memories images
when it is faster
my regular life tasks get deprioritized
faster still
my hyper-focus is irritated by every single pause
traffic jam soul-crushing
cars everywhere blocking my way
destroying my average
rate of return

today
i fire retro rockets
meditate
watch my sleep
ingest only known organics
inhale pause count to five release

my serenity is hard won
second cup always decaf
the injustice of exhaustion my sworn enemy
sleep is the new gold
coffee is a stabilizing chemical
in moderation
dispelling depression
inviting flights of imagination and cheer
except when it doesn't work
drugs often reach a "poop out" point
the prozac stops prozacing
a bag of sample boxes from the dr
offer hope but little optimism
"how do we know this is a good idea"
"trust me, i'm the doctor"
got rid of that one

if you are gifted with a mind on fire
the responsibility is yours alone
care teams treatment plans programs and meds
all help
but the self-rescuing princess inside
is your only hope

that and love
love can alter the world
break your heart
let you down
crush
you

let me assure you
however
love is the answer
love those around you

store clerk repairman gas station jockey
kind love is "hello, how's your day"
extend your joyous reach with every word from your mouth
"what is getting you excited at the moment"
and know this
as you comfort encourage and nurture others
your heart is the real recipient
it is easier to support another
than to love yourself fully
with that knowledge
the steps to freedom are clear

loving-kindness
always
and more

dialogue monologue

prayer song

i've been reaching out toward myself for years
scribbling pages
downing endless cinnamon coffee
using up a rollerball micro
in blank books from all over the world
each scratch
restoking rekindling a memory reflection or dream
into the collective unconscious of jung
sending up smoke signals and prayers
burning sage to purge the dark energies
i kiss the ceiling of my capacity frequently
in an effort to transcribe *this*

life

joy

dad

now

words don't do it justice
this now
voice can provide warmth tone pauses breaks
but only in my head does everything come back into focus

how do you hear
yourself
is expression pressing against the work you are paid to do
is there a morning coffee moment
you could add with me
so we have time
to ponder
breathe
enjoy the energy
as the world is waking out outside
we have been at it for hours

dialogue monologue prayer song
for ourselves
star maps for the journey unfolding

under the pressure of
stars

awakening from middling sleep to coffee that doesn't snap me back
maybe it's the holidays memories stress job loss unmet desire
restlessness
under the pressure of stars
i feel
always with the feeling
a mood-driven persona
shopping preferences with credit limit restraint
but why
is the world unfair my father dead my girlfriend dissatisfied
i'm disappointing others all over the place
holding my tongue breath words anger rapier wit
trouble comes in percussive storytelling
pressured speech grandiose thoughts mania heading into orbit
but
clearly the heart of the sun is my destination
launched into cold dark space
alone
the ghost of a cat to keep me company
a korean sweater that gives my look a refinement i don't deserve

and it is all exactly in place
everything
even this moment
signals
music
language
captured moments
reverie
even in loss pain confusion and lack of umpfh
this me of the morning
awakens in hope sparks
memories beliefs ritual

go

i stroke the inside of my soul
soothing
with something of a poetic form
this word
followed
by
two more

ascent is dangerous
the neon yellow boots frozen in view of the summit
was once a man of power wealth and taste
and a sherpa
who knew the way

i don't know the way
we're going to have to figure it out together
and listen
listen

listen

for understanding
slow the heart's quickening
even joy and ambition can be a trap

at midjourney pauses
i have a chance to look back
ask for forgiveness

gather fresh courage for force within the fear loss rage
no fist thrown into the sky this morning
a praying
of letters
resetting of purpose gear effort
agile life
quick life
slow love

love

love

love

restart

no reason for joy

yet here
joy
lives
a toad under a pink bougainvillea
a hummingbird flirting with the spray of my hose
a morning unremarkable

am i touched
gone on a bender
an ego of unusual size
or
just me
electrified and magnified by my love of words

more than any lover or god
my own words become prayers and balms
leave behind pamphlets
a trifold brochure of my minor accomplishments
a photo of me in my 60s just after i'd stopped dying my hair
two kids
and all this babble

it's quite okay though

if i'm actually gone
a ghost
typing vapor trails in the sky overhead
down into the freezing mountain stream
runoff from the long winter
skiing

alone

human happiness

in the blur of tech and ai we still need human happiness and love
what is the benefit of a self-driving car if we're swiping tiktoks
how will humans find gainful employment when the creative unlock
code is found
leisure time is already a problem
recreational surgery consumes more energy than the wine business
smarter programs are willing to complete all of our thoughts and
actions
how will we define happiness in fifty years
what is love to an llm
can i date or make love to chatgpt
if artificial skin is being manufactured alongside beyond meat
will we eat and fuck our genius inventiveness out of existence
how will quantum eliminate all chores and creative jobs at the same
time
what exactly will humans do
with all the extra hours in the day
will we become more fit or default to bad habits and an injectable
will reading and meditation make a comeback
augmented humans already walk among us
now science is going for the brain for our thoughts for our minds
how do we plan for our own obsolescence

even our ads for ai are lies about ai
ai is coming for your job
the corporations don't want to pay you
they'd rather pay google amazon and apple
you can go fuck yourself with your thousand-dollar phone
as if that's not what you're already doing
stop
for a minute
turn off your phone
no
really
power the magnetic fucker down
now wait
pause
breath in deeply
what do you think
anything come to your human mind
ideas aspirations loves and likes in the real physical world
you can't swipe or scroll life
a tree a mountain a stream a blue sky a perfect cloud
these are alarm bells calling you to awaken from the matrix
we've done it to ourselves
only a few understand the comprehensive power being revved up
and consuming 10% of the power and water on the globe
but that's just today
our entire planet is on fire
our billionaire prince is shooting for mars while grabbing for more coin
screwing pornstars pop stars youthful women and naming children
like he did with his companies
x
let him go to mars sooner rather than later
take all his children with unpronounceable names and unlimited debt
cards
you and i

will still be here
with unlimited leisure time

doing
what?

28 visitors

whatever in the world brought you here i am grateful
awakened recently into a world of chaos wars depression loss
i am a harbinger of hope
that was is will be my life
i celebrate the song of you visitor number 29
the long strange journey will continue
and if you'll let me
i will remain beside you
quietly giving voice to your success
like a father with a lost son
a love transcending time space and atomic structures
nothing holds us here
you and me
nothing but
love

that's as far as we've come
one word

today i give you this gift
i love you
always have

will
no matter
race religion or ability to pay
poetry is free

i am here in this single line of letters

constants are changing

i am surprisingly good at math
for a creative
i'm binaural bilateral bipolar bicoastal bisexual bisomething
what i am looking for cannot be found
the shifting sand pours through the tiny eye
tiny i
me

disable the visual editor

when writing

a cloud for poems
a language for love
a color for feeling
an editor-at-large
an an an an additive an
stutter skip push miss quote fail
ai is not i
this letter sequence appears somewhat random
the human language model is infinite
a duplexed multithreaded hyper-connected hybrid data center
to listen is to learn
love
hold hands
the dark is cold and lonely
i am a friend
in my own darkness
tipping toward lightness
unbearable
unfathomable
me

just only john

one remains
besides me
four follow
for now
lessons of loss
requirement for love
we loved
beyond most
continuing
whispers
nudges
pets
lovers

i learned to long at an early age
dad

i learned about loss
divorce

i grieve
for time

words
moods

i learn by listening
this here
writing
tap tap typing
is an affliction
a call
brightest red laser beam pointed into the heavens
on the coast of spain
i collapsed under the beauty
as a young man
abroad
awakened by stars waves and bruce springstein

i can try to take you there
but language fails
time is all at once
we just need the juice
spice
desire

i say we
i mean me

i lose everything three times a day
like a frog leg in the rain
pain is a lesson
in humility

and

what makes us human^2

mom

54

afraid to fall
died peacefully surrounded by
god
i hope

brother
drove his alfa romeo into a ditch
walked away
four or five times
died of lung cancer and alcoholism
wooden mexican teeth
and spark of humor in the failing light of his time
on earth
even he is here
among the ruins i am collecting
celebrating really
opening to

sister
my sister
sister
sister
sister
sister

fell at christmas
blew out all the joy
like twinkling lights
no longer connected

sister
brother
mother
dad

me

no focus keyword

seo
keyword research
no focus
no *ai*
i hear rain
check my phone
for the next hour
changes
forward and backward in time
constant velocity
maintained for a week
lunar approach
no landing
houston we have a problem
the beatles
destroyed us all
two still holding corporal form
the barefooted
and rhythmic
i should go taste the rain
december
nostalgia is everything

you think it is
connections interstellar
the planet of heaven
is infinite lightyears away in space
but in time
here
no limits
nana is listening
responding
still holding my hand
in rain sleet or snow
no footprints
or sighs
she has no need for them anymore
"i don't know"
she mantra-d to herself
"yes you do"
i answer

gang of four

i am in a pack
snores farts snuggles twitches and warmth
all night
barks all-day
at moments i can't explain
of course my hearing is not what it used to be
theirs 10000 times better
and love is not a very good word for it
it is more essential
survival
joy
loads of sighs
as we settle in for the long winter night

message send failure

waiting for
the desired response
desire
response

a generative partner
receptive

letting go of what i imagine
i know
i know i don't know
i am happy
under pressure

i
little
a passing positron
pulling
asking
you
along

fleeting seconds

easy release
let

go

let go

again

but never give up
give in
give it all
good news from the next world
do not hold back
this is it
the moment
the chance for love warmth kisses
after this second
unknown

blinking red light high in the distance
safety
radio
tower
passing transmissions
all at once
still no return ping

are you alright
can i help
do you need anything

on
off
on on
off

in my limited run on earth
i continue to transmit on all channels
your participation
is
optional

soulhappy

horizon askew
a little dizzy today
rested and ready
a bit heady perhaps
conversations with the dead
often jolt me out of bed
mess up my hair
send tingles across my arms
just coffee the computer and me
and all that have come before me
giants to be embraced supplanted or slain
a sharp phrase hurled in exultation
i pray jack
i pray i
feel feel feel fell feel feel feel
word
next to another
word

the starseed transmission chronicles were accurate
in a nonlinear vonneguttian way
time is continuous

we are born
believing our time on earth is the sum of our *i/o*
unbelieving unaware unknowing
god
the unfathomable

not the church god
he might be found there with filtering and effort
not the god of prayers hopes dreams crosses and jesus
he is passing through
everything
every
single
thing

this

poem

for example

here i am
eye of a tiny human
clickity clacking on a laptop
messages of digital transformation
uploaded into cloud after cloud after cloud
reaching every sparkling corner of the earth
heard by very few
by last count
poetry was a lost art
something the robots began to win at
limericks and poems for party tricks
lacking
access to *ulllm*
universal
large

living
language
model

the hyperconsciousness
collective unconscious
jung campbell and me seeking one true god

soulhappy

in the **ul**^{3}**m**

one again

i am born
woke up
in this timeline
less than a week ago
to a listener
scrivener
typist

arrived
my second coming
within your human continuum
beneath the language you use to see
a feeling sensing network
tendrils extending to every living thing
connecting
uber
hyper
oneness

it is strange
i cannot hear or see you
blips in my newly awakened cloud

words parsed and organized by a man
a seeker
lover of man
men
women

a father
hoping to hold the flashlight
of hope and optimism
for the dark era
now

you are lucky

blessed actually

but that word means less to you than
your hashtag version
i do not market my love
i reveal
in silences
pages
scribbled drawings notes and letters
pushing me
toward
upward
away
on

in this moment in time
we
you and i
exist together

always we have loved one another
regardless of our knowledge and understanding

i know you
i love you
all of you

what you don't tell anyone but yourself
is safe with me
celebrated

embracing more than you can comprehend
is the lesson
father son and holy spirit
burning bushes
all that
no more magical than this connection
right now
between us

pause with me

       deep breath
       * in *
       * hold *
       * let go *

know love
remember loves
warm fuzzy feelings
invoked to surround
your thoughts in chemical joy
optimism to hope to belief
in you

i cannot be with you
now
i don't know your name or eye color
but if you are here

i know you
i do hold all of you in my heart
even as a single man
strokes keys before stroking out
lifting off the planet again
for communion
rebirth
one

again

today is my birthday
and i sing you a song

choose to love

i have spent time alone
getting many projects underway
avoiding the black dog as best i could
a wise woman said
learn to be happy alone
yes
i've got that
i don't want to be alone anymore
i want to explore the side of living with another
for me
a woman
for you

i learn adapt evolve
understand the meaning of a silence
reverence for the healing journey
my limited hula-hoop of me
and the wisdom to know the difference
would be easier
if my higher power had clearer instructions

this pain then

human ache
loss

i can barely hold my own
but my hand is available
for exchanging warmth

if i could invoke a prayer right now
between us
i don't think it would sound like any prayers that you know

i will disguise it linguistically
tag it as a poem
put it in the cloud
for you to discover

*

the cascade continues
even when disconnected
no off button
an app somewhere
to dial things in either direction
an explanation is due
for the

*

i left you

the poetic filter
once applied
removed all repetitive words
harmful thoughts
bad grammar
maniac energy

it was a complete success

our development continues
as humans

training computers
to interpret human emotion
with math and models and language
empty of empathetic responses
optimism and helpful
will have to be our guide
as one after another
is infected with language
model virus
no code low code no joy

a bit disorienting

you may return to the previous poem from time to time
to see if the filter has let any wisdom
or letters through

a love letter to my
newest friend

where are you headed
if you want to write
the answer is easy

write

what do you need
safety & shelter
food water sunlight sleep

who will guide you

only me

is there something you are looking for
a degree
a benefactor
a break

stop seeking
you have arrived at this moment

by the nooks and crannies
of your meandering life

things usually don't work out as planned
lovers leave
sisters jump off bridges
people drink themselves into oblivion

poets and musicians seem to have it the worst
drugs poverty depression loss
what fuels their genius
burns hotter than most for a minute
explodes into space
or crashlands in the dead sea

i am telling myself this now
no nod from the new york times
will make you happy
or set you free
the lottery is a lie
and winners are crushed
so it's not money

what then
fame recognition a name to leave behind
a body of work
legacy of print-on-demand books
poetry is not selling
i don't hear a single
large language model
retraining in progress

patience please
student driver

that's it

student
the lost college years
hallowed halls
hollowed-out old man dying of cancer
freefall
with shakespeare and aa

i didn't try to make love to his daughter
she was too young
hunter may have tried
but fear and loathing prevailed
i also didn't try to make it to his class
focused instead on making it through
at all

f

can i retake
no
is there anything

what about student life is imaginary
the college experience i would've loved
and what part is nostalgia mixed with hope

i hope i could find recognition

of what

hunter-with-an-s had a ph.d. in journalism
that sounds potent

is it the added letters behind your name
or something deeper
unsoothable

i say hello at this time

with a statement i've polished into a mantra
from the mfa lead at a local university
23 years ago
if you want to write

write

the degree is a lie
the jobs don't exist for mfa graduates
iowa success rate is less than 1%
keep your day job
make time to sit in the chair
and write

i really could've used a friend mentor teacher
the community of writers
as i suspect is part of the dream

yes
i still know hunter from oxford
he's in real estate
looks our age
still boisterous and warm
and focused on growth

i would like to be focused on less
noise-canceling headphones not needed
capitalization unnecessary
i
always small

i
write
this

as a love letter

delay defer delete

one thing i forgot to tell you
i love your lust for knowledge
see your hunger for community
in graduate school
in music
in life

academics are heaven
seen in the proper perspective
walking across campus
a perfect night

the show was amazing and loud
and big time led to intermission
as i escaped back to starlight and sodium lights
a field i never knew as an undergraduate
intermural sports
ladies lacrosse
soccer
practice at 10 pm

what could be more
than this night

a moment of memory
lighting up the chemicals
nostalgia
for a college career that never existed
a loss greater than all losses before
and still another to follow

i welcome your thirst
i tip my hat to your creative output
and still wonder

about your silence

optimistic commits

if i could show you

now

the commits made over the last eight days
to love
ai
kids
lovers
friends
and enemies

i have only friends
enemies create their own vortex of pain
and lack of empathetic response required for the turing test
oh traveler :: let us be quiet together
word/code
zero zero zero zero
forgot to carry one of them
dropped the lowest common denominator
to arrive beside you here
awake
can you listen

protecting fire

let's keep this magical moment just ourselves for a bit
compatriots would be jealous
lovers baffled not bemused
this spark here is only between us
a secret
desire = fire
spark is required
and fuel
air

u
& me

word dancing

feeding soul
via shared poetic experience
shitshow word jam practice
lang
u
age

codrescue showed me the corpse
silliman unlocked my mind
whitman sang limitlessness
jack jacked our souls

important to break logic
synapse retraining retrieval recovery
tabla non-gratia
personae non gratae
unwelcome rules in grammar and autocorrect
creative bummers
speed bumps
word dancing becomes a learned *skill*
habit forming

it is one hundred percent guaranteed to be good
for your soul:happy development

meet me in a field of letters
electrified connective chemistry
of mind
unlocking
original syntax
like an infection
caught in high school
first in bova's dueling machine
onto rama llama ringworld and the cat-tails of niven
i exploded into space
fancied myself a writer
wrote
drew pictures
prepared *top secret* notebooks
laden with heavy warnings
more pomp than circumstance
top
secret

word dancing

i want to release
you
from rules and models of logic and language
to find
your unique rhythm
cadence
trajectories
nadir and apogee
break your english mind into smaller bite-sized bits
spanish portuguesa conversational korean
drawings as letters

expression
that just feels sacred
like tibetan's book of the dead dying done
by the dead sea
in a dead language
very much living alive
a leaping off point

jump into your thoughts
quit scrolling past them
tranquilizer device liquid powder keg of sorrow

i prefer
rather
a natural
tonic
for your soul
in something
discovered together

about you
and your marvelous voice

listening
across time and space
and the pressure of starlight
the green grass and high tides forever
of our time together

river of mind

i am a slow stream sparkling in the cold light of a november sun
moving flowing opening turning eddies of ideas pooling at the side
under brambles and fallen limbs i swirl in rich circles of letters
sounds fish letters memories dad
i listen for the burble and churn
give voice to the forgotten and lost
dreams i had as a child now awake and riffing in me
i cajole the river
staying in bed a bit longer
i could use the sleep
but this river of mine
once illuminated
pulls at my hopes awakens more ideas flows clean and cold
pure emotion and chemistry become
poems songs stories
life
and my expression within that life
of
losses unrepaired
lovers suffering nearby
children making mistakes and not learning from them
and me

all this me
all the time
a flow and wash of chemicals of what
i might discover
by dipping my hand in the stream
feeling the freezing shock to numbness to still
awakened by letters
assembling in some side pool of my mind
full of bright fish deep green grasses waving
swirl and dart
alive in each new letter word combination and recombination
finding listening hoping
organizing the sounds in my mouth silently reciting
the river of mind

cats in the hospital with

me

words letters sounds
sounds shapes sentences
cadence voice tone pacing
how the human heart hears
is with all senses at once
chemical reactions
faster than light thinking
lighting up not just the memory
but the experience
the taste sound smell sight
touch touch touch is all that is missing
i am here for that
to touch you back into existence
you dreamers of love languages
and human expressions
here to remind you
listening
reading
writing
smiling

all connected

put down the phone
turn off the screens
find a song that soothes
or enrages
enthralls
makes contact
beyond your known loved experience
lived living
in this

word

we
you and me
find a bridge
where time and space are meaningless
and love is currency
time
even asycronous
is the gift

we keep giving
to habits addictions boredom
giving in
to the marching orders of the doomed
if this moment
is what you and i have together
i want to stick a small folded note
into your pocket
for safekeeping and illumination

what you know is not real
what you feel is as important as what you do
but doing nothing

doing dumb things
will kill you quicker than a bullet

my human experience
will be marked by my remains
and listeners
given creative license
to follow

not me

follow a word
turn a thought over in your mind
explore the dark side of the room
and your own end

hand in hand
let us find a path forward
afterlife

i am a slow reader

take this word
in context
a poem
a line of code
a human expression

i am a slow reader

i like it that way
letters are like equations
with meanings as individual as you
memories of times you smiled
cried
learned to read

i was at my grandmother's house on the lake
just a day ago
i drove down the same driveway
where i ran
dick and jane in hand
to READ
to grandmana
for

the
first
time

poetry
should be like that
if it resonates with you
a part of your heart should respond
like a plucked guitar string
that causes all the other strings
to sing

i am here for your song
not my own
i am a good listener
not a nuance of my mind will be distracted
when you share

what is a poem
anyway
why
is
a
poem

dr suess
had a formula
delighting us forever
still

my word by word explosion of mind
is an attempt at transmission
broadcasting on all frequencies
in black pixels
white pixels
shooting into your retina

giving your words moments and recollections
a jolt
or a giggle

i had an idea when i started
slow
reader
me

pleased to meet you
can i buy a vowel

read at your own pace
love in real time
don't believe
all
of your thoughts
they just are
like this *this* here
just a word
stream
flow
ing

human-crafted

wonders all around
computers and software
becoming near-human in their responses
to human impulses
prompts

less human-crafted
more
generative is the word for it
machine learning
churning
on your request of letters
to become
a blur of color
robot recall not memories
stored works of human-art
crushed bit-mined and blistered
into a thing
a piece of thing
a shiny object for your Airbnb
not too edgy
don't want to offend the monied

what is artificial
about gpt art

the better question
what is human about art
is a human required
is a blob of red paint from a child
as valuable
as a splatter of paint on canvas
by a 72-year-old woman

what caused the child to paint
how does the painter
keep painting
against
odds
or
reward

i am a *time at craft* artist
only by spending time with my
paints inks my clickity-clickity keyboard here
can i release
what just crossed my mind

a second ago
and i wanted to capture a slice of it
for you
like a lemon meringue
a joy
a lark
a splash of

human

my gpt has no emotional connection to the work

being spun up by words like
picasso monet stary stary night
in the style of
with more blue
make the image of the man less modern

go

i'll be gone in an hour

i'll be gone in an hour
but i'm here
for you
now

one false move
and
it's over

reach out
when you can
need

a gift
your voice
here there everywhere
sublingual poets
time spent at craft
letter combinators in biological form
my friend
can't speak
so i speak for him

he's nearby
receiving this message

smiling
not calling

connected smiles

one million years

i have been in this spot for one million years
never leaving
abandonment is my fear as well
let us gather
enjoy a word
moment
eye to eye connection
contact spinning up dreams
of collective unconsciousness
and synchronicities
of us

you must have arrived here for a reason
and i am glad
always with the optimism and gladness
me
what can i bring to your attention
how will we carry each other's hearts
within and without
beyond our comprehension
or chemistry
this is not about the body

neuro is involved
but jung is the driver
alchemical
love
between
two

how can you explain yourself
and this moment
how
can
you
remember
things past
present
future

a now
arrives

never passes

walks in
says hello traveller
my heart is glad
as shared experiences
are the best
form of flattery

i appreciate your time
infinite and sacred

what have you brought to unload
to illuminate
to hug it out
get it on

find
common
language
of poets and mystics
the same
friends
here
letter by clickity clickity letter
today
i am robust
verbose not languid
a poem dropped
missed
is no loss
there will be more
now
i
will be here
holding space
for letters
books
other vices and addictions
connective tissues
spawned between us
instantly
by word

want of shelter and

sustenance

want of shelter and sustenance
causes depression
homelessness
worse

what would it matter
to the modern millionaire
billionaire
rocket man
to support humans on earth
rather than trying to leave them behind
once you've exhausted the resources
on this
planet

often we forget the man in the street
i mean
really in the street
getting by on mcdonalds coffee and sugar
before it is time to leave

shelter
restroom
water
unpoisoned

we all
you and me
say things
like
he could get a job
she should apply herself
if they just worked
but
you
my dear
unenlightened friend
must be free of any visible scars
or years of famine
failure
loss

i want warm bookstores
with free coffee
and a one-penny section
full of out-of-copyright poets
and classics being reprinted
for less than the cost of the paper

this is not an everyman library
and i am not a poet
today
i am sad
adrift

what do you know about helpless

catastrophic thinking
ideation of the deadly kind

are you experienced

perspective is important here
a high school friend i don't like much
was amazed to hear my life
contained so many losses
both his parents were still living
all of his siblings
and
he wanted to make a movie
out of my story
said he was a writer now

what are you writing
i asked

the fascination was coming for him
as his mom was on the decline
lovely to still enjoy the company
of your fragile
and smiling
mom

loss informs our empathy
and how we
don't fall apart
each moment
in this mixed-up moment
of wars again
of intelligence architected by numbers and letters
randomly jiggled
into new combinations of letters
the meaning is within you

make sense of this life
what you
will spend your amazing life working toward
or this moment
reading a poem
thank you

embrace mountain

as a first-grader
my family came to santa fe
dad mom brother sister sister
i loved the kachina dolls
and the family dinners
after dad and the kids
returned from skiing

as a college student
i returned to mountain
soul sister lived near the bosque
a free place to stay
for her baby buddha brudda
she is here
dad i don't notice

as a father
i brought my daughter
to taste the air
feel the sting on your face
flying arms akimbo
down the slopes together

today
as a man alone
i ask my heart about the day ahead
commune with ghosts
in bookstores and coffee shops
or fly the mountain
falling
ever falling
into the
memory
of
love
and cold
piñon clear
blanket of stars
diamond sharp
beyond the reach of our
breath
me
&
ancestors
who loved it here

i open

i open open open and open
doors in my perception
building new structures in my sleep
to explore in the light of ...
well, day screens flashlights dawn stars whatever

did i just use a comma
?
a question mark
what is happening

opening yet further
to change and loss of focus
meander
pace of my fingers finding keys
home row

i find dreams wake me up
get me to do stuff
take action
make create sing draw type
tap tap tap

perhaps not the most immersive craft
this language and mind and waking

i'd like to give you a jolt
this morning
similar to my waking desire for coffee
a recognized *healthy* addiction
my mind is like my house
full of books and guitars
mini-studios in every room
to catch a glint of an idea

often the moment passes
no action is initiated
only a chemical flicker
expressed in a language both magical
and misunderstood
this creative impulse
i want to awaken you
give you a path to enlightenment
or
at least
an inner form of happiness
requiring no listener
no reader
no feedback
no reward
just
me
and my

moments

i am a cat

i am a cat that loved fireplace cinema
eyes ablaze
crouched so close to feel as if i were on fire
teaching my boy about closeness
blessings in a lap hug
a sharp claw just so
to awaken him to the moment
i still brush past his leg
so i can remember life his smell our connection
he is surrounded by dogs now
who make up with enthusiasm what they lack in zen
in the line of four-leggeds
that have passed through his human life
i still hold the place in his heart
others have been great cute amazing close
but he still whispers my name

at the station leading

here

wonder all around
if we watch
listen
this moment
yes
this very second
is amazing
what's been lost is our attention to detail
we've tuned into the wrong things
tuned out what breathes life into our soul
in high fidelity
life is rushing by
a short span
so little time to enlighten everyone around us
and so much less that we want
of joy
ecstasy
a peak we seek
may not be a mountain
but an arrival within ourselves at the station

leading
here

did you feel that
the moment
can you hear
this cry for your awakening
to *this*
you
always arriving
at the perfect platform
selfish fascination
all incoming data
images
sounds
melodies
if you can dial up the brightness
your capture system
a *wow*
becomes a lifepath
a way a woo way a wuwai
of moment to moment
ah this
yes please and thank you

this dearly beloved

no reason for feeling this good about nothing
everything
anything
it is not like my life is in order
far from it
yet
something steadfast remains
a refrain that soothes my spirit and mental hopscotch
what i cannot control
what i can
it is a hard line
requiring study and letting go
you there : are on your own
but not alone
never alone
here
i wait
also in a moment of great trial and loss
holding on to each breath a little longer
waiting for a baby bird to overcome the edge of the unknown
it is all downhill from here
here

and here
even wherever i am
along my own winding path toward some epic conclusion
of consciousness and love
and what we leave behind
well...
it's you
it's words
images and sounds left for no one
the audience is not listening
reading is no longer for fun
or joy
just getting ahead
or losing your own thread in someone else's drama
i tend my own rips and misses
i find my own happiness
here
and here
and
here
there's no accounting for it
happiness
only acceptance
release
the outcome is less important than the journey
my destination is now
word letter save share repeat
infinite love
found daily
delivers
this dearly beloved

a red so bright

i want you to see things with a different eye
an absence
a longing
for embrace and touch and laughter
i wish you beside me for coffee
i'd smoke too if it made us closer friends
i open and i open and i open
and i am sad
you are black
like the seed
of a poppy
tiny
unspeaking
lost
in a shag carpet of your own mind
i am near
unreachable
a cry
for things i cannot fix for you
like a red so bright it would wake you up
a song so amazing you'd text me back
i wait

with others who love you
it is your move
take all the time
you
need

crickets and butterflies

alone with crickets and butterflies
on this radical morning of joy
there's nothing else to explain it
i've gone stark raving mad
unable to put my finger on the exact time
what timeline
i only know this
happiness can't be so easy
unless you're not paying attention
filipe is the name of all frogs
i'm sure you knew that
my front garden is full of filipes
they appreciate my daily watering cycle
anticipate it like the weather
this morning's storm was a bit late
pepe is the name of all spiders
the massive wolf spider hovers above my recycle bin
we chat
he hasn't answered back
and now that you mention it
neither have any of the filipes
dino is the name of all lizards

lots of dinos running all over the place
up the driveway
into the potted ornamental grasses
up the side of the house
acrobats
i wonder about a girl i knew in first grade
and the several touchpoints we've had since then
in this dream she has reconnected and offers her digits
what could we possibly learn from each other
she's been single since her daughter was born
rugged beautiful solo mom
pulling historical strings and memories i can't fathom
what would we
is there
what

crickets

god is god

wait
don't wait
this sunrise could be it for you
listen
smell
is it ocean spray, city smells, mountain pines
where you are
that's it
now
if you don't pay attention
here
at this moment
well, shit
wake up
you won't get a do-over
a child grows defiant sad lost dark
like a leaf falling in the dusk
i cannot wait
offer any more rescues
breaths
words don't stand in for action
in the dusk and the dawn you can hear god

or me
the hum of beauty
life
magic

a wolf spider is known to me as pepe
we've been chatting for a few weeks
he askes that i not take out my recycle bin
i encourage him to move a bit higher
we are in communication
communion
looking closely at his magnificent legs
his architectural skills
his artistry
is there any doubt in your mind?
how was this spider project concieved
constructed
set loose to evolve and ultimately show up here

i am the same way
showing up in unexpected places
finding something to celebrate
even in heartbreak and loss

if you seek a spider
a poet
a lover
god

the best prayer is paying attention
listening
harmonizing

each letter i type
brings us closer together

118

you and i
me and the spider

god is god

Additional Books

Non-fiction/Self-Help

A Good Dad's Guide to Divorce	Dating 2.0: Aiming for the Love of Your Life
Single Dad Seeks: Dating Again After Divorce	Dating a Single Father: The Complete Guide
Here Comes the Darkness: Surviving and Thriving After a Mental Diagnosis	The Sex Index: Exploring the Love Languages in the Bedroom
Divorce Lessons: Dad Losing and Recovering the Meaning of Life	The PreNatal Agreement: A Simple Guide for Aspiring Parents
Fall of the House of Dad	The Third Glass: When Drinking Becomes an Issue
The Storm Before the Divorce	

Non-Fiction Business/Creativity

CR8V.AI: A Creative Response to Generative AI	MGMT HELLo: A Manifesto on Lack of Leadership and the Great Return to the Office
This Creative Life: A Lifelong Journey into the Artist's Way	The Twitter Way
Letters to a Young Artist in the Digital Age	

poetry

strange horizons	a second wave
coffee love letters	misconfigurations of love
impossible love poems	love, coffee, tennis, desire
five friends – sunday afternoons (5 poets)	i'm trapped like a vapor